BRIAN TRACY

New York Times bestselling author of *Eat That Frog!*

The POWER of FOCUS

BULL'S-EYE

simple **truths**

LEAD TO CHANGE

an imprint of Sourcebooks, Inc.

Photo Credits
Cover: front, phipatbig/Shutterstock
Internals: pages i, vii, 9, 23, 35, 46, 52, 65, 67, 71, 84, 93, 97, 101, phipatbig/Shutterstock; page 14, All Vectors/Shutterstock; page 63, Lynn Harker/Sourcebooks

Published by Simple Truths, an imprint of Sourcebooks, Inc.
P.O. Box 4410, Naperville, Illinois 60567–4410
(630) 961–3900
Fax: (630) 961–2168
www.sourcebooks.com

Printed and bound in the United States of America.
WOZ 10 9 8 7 6 5 4 3 2 1

Table of Contents

Introduction: Hitting Your Target v

1: The Power of Clarity 1

2: The Power of Focus 11

3: The Power of Purpose 25

4: The Power of Concentration 37

5: The Power of Excellence 51

6: The Power of People 69

7: The Power of Persistence 87

About the Author 103

Hitting Your Target

We are living in the greatest time in all of human history. Despite short-term economic fluctuations, there have never been more opportunities for more people to achieve more of their goals than there are today.

The fact is, you have more potential than you could use in a hundred lifetimes. And the more of your potential you use, the more potential becomes available to you. The more you learn, the more you can learn.

There is no reason for you not to be earning twice as much as you are today, or even five times and ten times as much. There are people all around you who are no more talented than you, and no better educated, who are already earning this much. And what others have done, you can do as well, if you just learn how.

Clarity, Focus, and Concentration

You have the ability right now to achieve more than you ever have before, as long as you incorporate three essential mental skills into your life: clarity, focus, and concentration.

You must become absolutely clear about who you are and what you want. You must focus on your most important goals and activities. And finally, you must concentrate single-mindedly until you have completed your tasks and achieved your goals.

These are the three essential requirements practiced by all successful people throughout history to accomplish extraordinary results and great achievements.

Fortunately, each of these skills is learnable with practice and repetition. Just as you can develop your physical muscles through hard work and concentration, you can develop your mental muscles through continuous repetition.

Your aim in life should be to achieve all of the wonderful things that are possible for you. You want to score big—to hit the *bull's-eye*, the center of the target—in everything you do.

In the pages ahead, you'll learn how to unleash your powers for success and accomplish more in the next few months than many people do in a lifetime. Let's begin.

ACCOMPLISH more in the next few months than many people do in a lifetime.

CHAPTER ONE

The Power of Clarity

On November 13, 1899, a remarkable man named Howard Hill was born in Pennsylvania. He enjoyed sports and was excellent at baseball and football. He soon realized that, although he was talented in those sports, he did not have the ability to excel and become a champion player. So he turned his attention to *archery*, a sport that was not as competitive as others.

Archery turned out to be the perfect sport for Howard Hill. Over the years, he won 196 consecutive archery championships when most people would have been happy to win one or two titles. He became the finest archer in the world. He developed his own long bow so he could shoot farther and with greater accuracy.

With this skill, he became the greatest hunter with a bow and arrow in history. At archery competitions, it was naturally assumed by everyone that Howard Hill would be number one. The other competitors only hoped for the number two, three, or four spots.

You Could Defeat the Best

But even though Howard Hill was the finest archer in the world, you could have beaten him with a bow and arrow with your current skill level as long as one condition existed: he couldn't see the target.

Imagine Howard Hill went to an archery competition—but there was a sheet or a blanket hanging somewhere in front of the target so he could not see where it was. All the talent and experience in the world of archery would do him no good if the target was covered. As Zig Ziglar said, "The fact is that you can't hit a target that you can't see."

It is the same with you. Unless you are perfectly clear about what you want—your target, and the bull's-eye on that target—you will never be able to win championships in the great contest of life.

What Is Your Target?

According to Lewis Carroll, "If you don't know where you are going, any road will get you there."

Thomas Carlyle once wrote, "A person with a clear purpose will make progress on even the roughest road. A person with no purpose will make no progress on even the smoothest road."

The greater clarity you have about who you are—your likes and dislikes, what you want, your goals and objectives—the greater progress you will make under even the most difficult of circumstances.

What is the most valuable and important work you do? When I first heard this question, I was not sure about the answer. Then I discovered that it was *thinking!*

Thinking is the highest paid work you do because of the concept of *consequences.* This concept says that something is important to the degree to which it has serious potential consequences. Something is unimportant to the degree to which it has minor or no potential consequences.

Determine the Consequences

In time management, one of the best ways to set priorities is to think about the likely consequences of doing or not doing a task. Successful people are those who spend most of their time on tasks and activities that have big potential consequences. They can have a real impact or influence on the future. Unsuccessful, unhappy people instead spend most of their time doing things of little or no consequence at all.

Of all the things you can do, the quality of your thinking has the greatest consequences of all. The quality of your thinking determines the quality of your choices and decisions. Your choices and decisions determine the actions you take. And the actions you take determine the quality and quantity of your results.

In life and work, results are everything. In the final analysis, you will be judged by the results you accomplish, for yourself and others. And the quality of your results will largely be determined by the quality of the thinking that preceded the actions you take.

The Law of Probability

Your goal should be to achieve the highest levels of success possible in every area of your life that is important to you. Fortunately, you have tremendous control over what happens to you and what you accomplish. By doing certain things in a certain way, over and over, you can dramatically increase the likelihood that you are going to enjoy high income and live an exciting life. There is a much higher probability that you will hit your personal bull's-eyes.

Here is an example. The Law of Probability says there is a probability that everything can happen and that these probabilities can be calculated with tremendous accuracy. One of the greatest discoveries is that you can increase the probability of success in any field by doing more of the things other successful people do.

Hitting the Bull's-Eye

Imagine a game of darts and a dartboard. The bull's-eye on the dartboard is worth fifty points. Each of the outer rings is worth ten points less—forty points, thirty points, twenty points, ten points, and then no points at all.

Imagine a dart thrower. He has little skill with darts. He is in a bar and has had a couple of drinks. The light is poor. The dartboard is thirty or forty feet away. Nonetheless, he starts throwing dart after dart.

Because of the Law of Probability, if he keeps throwing darts, even under the worst conditions, he will eventually hit the target somewhere.

Hoping for the Best

If he continues throwing darts, assuming an unlimited supply, hour after hour, day after day, week after week, and year after year, he might eventually hit a bull's-eye.

Many people live their lives like that. They wish and hope and dream about a "big score." They try a dozen or a hundred different things. They keep throwing darts at the dartboard of life. But eventually, most people give up and simply settle for mediocrity. They conclude that they are "not good enough" and that they will never have the skill and ability to hit a bull's-eye in the game of life.

Increase the Probabilities

But what if this same player takes a different strategy? What if he becomes really serious about hitting a bull's-eye and winning in the game of life? He hires an expert at the game of darts and takes some of the best training available to a person in this sport. Instead of being distracted, tired, and having a couple drinks, he is instead well-rested and clearheaded. The dartboard is well-lit and only a few feet away.

Now, what are his chances of hitting the target? They are much better because of his preparation and positioning.

What if he also has an endless supply of darts and continues to throw the darts, measuring and calibrating his accuracy with each throw, correcting his stance and his throwing, and persistently throws darts over and over again?

Winning Is Predictable

Under these conditions, the chance is almost 100 percent that he will eventually hit a bull's-eye. And once he hits a bull's-eye, if he continues to practice and improve his aim, he will eventually be able to hit bull's-eye after bull's-eye in the great game of life.

It is the same with you. You can dramatically increase your chances of hitting your bull's-eyes in life if you do the same things that champions do in your field, over and over.

The key is clarity. You must develop absolute clarity about who you are, what you really want, and the steps you will have to take to achieve what you want to achieve and to get to where you want to go.

You must do everything possible to increase the probability that you will be a big success in life. This brings us to the next exercise in hitting your bull's-eye: goals.

"The fact is that you can't hit a target that you can't **SEE**."

~ Zig Ziglar

CHAPTER TWO

The Power of Focus

"Success is goals, and all else is commentary."
—*Lloyd Conant*

Hitting your bull's-eye in life requires that you know exactly what it is and where it is. Your selection of a major definite purpose, the one goal that is more important to you than any other, is the starting point of massive success.

The goal-setting process is both simple and powerful—and potentially life changing. It consists of seven steps:

Step One

Decide exactly what you want. Imagine that you have no limitations. Imagine that you have all the talent and ability, all the knowledge and skill, all the contacts and relationships, and all the money and resources you need to achieve any goal you really want in life.

Practice *no limit thinking*. Forget about the past and whatever problems or limitations you may have had. Think instead about the future. Your future is limited only by your own imagination, and since your imagination has no limits, your future is unlimited as well.

Be Specific

1. Be specific about what you want. This will separate you from more than 80 percent of the population who, generally speaking, have no clear idea what they want.

2. Albert Einstein once said, "If you can't explain it simply, you don't understand it well enough."

3. If you ask people "Do you have goals?" they will always say something like "Of course I have goals!"

4. But when you ask them what their "goals" are, they will say things like "I want to be rich," "I want to be thin," "I want to be happy," "I want to have a nice house, car, and clothes," "I want to travel."

5. But these are not goals. These are wishes or fantasies. A wish is a goal with no energy behind it.

People Don't Set Goals

The great tragedy is that most people think they already have goals when all they really have are wishes. As a result, they never sit down to establish clear, specific goals for themselves. Because of this, they seldom accomplish even a fraction of what is truly possible for them.

Step Two

Write it down. Make it measurable. Only 3 percent of adults have written goals, and these people, according to studies done at Yale and Harvard, eventually earn ten times as much as people without goals.

The very act of writing down your goals moves you into the top 3 percent of adults living today. Writing down your goals activates the Law of Attraction and begins attracting into your life the people, ideas, and resources that will help you move toward the goals and to start the goals moving toward you.

Step Three

Set a deadline. Tell your subconscious computer exactly when you want to achieve your goal. Your subconscious mind loves deadlines, "forcing systems," that enable your mind to work twenty-four hours a day to bring the goal into your life.

If it is a big enough goal, set smaller deadlines. If it is a one-year goal, break it down into one-month goals, even one-week goals.

What if you don't achieve your goal by the deadline? Simple—set another deadline, and another and another if necessary. Remember, there are no unrealistic goals—only unrealistic deadlines.

Sometimes you will achieve the goal before you expect to, sometimes after. But you must have a target and a timeline to follow.

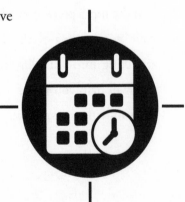

Step Four

Make a list. Write down everything you will have to do to achieve your goal. Identify the additional knowledge and skills you will require. Identify the obstacles you will have to overcome. Identify the people whose help you will require.

This part of the process is very important. When you set a big goal for yourself—to double your income or to achieve financial independence, for example—it can seem so overwhelming at first that you can become discouraged before you even begin.

But when you write out a list of all the individual tasks and activities you can engage in to achieve the goal, your goal starts to become more believable and achievable. You start to think, "I may not be able to achieve this entire goal, but I can do this one thing, and then this other thing."

Henry Ford once said, "Nothing is particularly hard if you divide it into small jobs."

Keep adding ideas and activities to your list until your list is complete.

Step Five

Organize the list into a plan. Just as you would plan any project, organize your list by sequence and priority.

Your *sequence* of activities refers to what you do first, what you do second, and what you do third to achieve your goal. Make a checklist to work from. Organize every activity, from the first to the last, just as you would with any worthwhile project. The use of a checklist to achieve your goal will increase the likelihood of success by ten times or more.

Organize your list by *priority* as well. Use the 80/20 Rule, which says that 20 percent of the items on your list will account for 80 percent of the value of the results you accomplish.

Once you have a written list of activities organized by sequence and priority, you have a plan you can use to accomplish almost any goal you can set for yourself. A person with a goal and a plan is like an archer or a dart thrower with everything they need to step up to the line and hit a bull's-eye.

Step Six

Take action on your list of activities. Do something. Do anything. As Einstein said, "Nothing happens until something moves."

Nothing happens until you move as well. Take the first step. The key to success has always been to have courage, overcome the inertia most people have, and simply take the first step.

Take Action

When you take the first step on the path to your goal, three wonderful things happen simultaneously. First, you immediately get feedback that enables you to make course corrections, assuring that you are moving the fastest way possible toward your goal.

Second, when you take the first step, you immediately get more ideas for additional actions that you can take to move ahead faster.

Third, when you take the first step, your self-confidence increases immediately. You feel more positive and powerful. Your self-esteem and self-respect go up.

You feel stronger and more capable of achieving even more goals.

You Can Always See the First Step

Once you have set a goal, you can always see the first step. And when you have the courage to take the first step, the second step will appear. When you take the second step, the third step will appear. You can achieve the biggest goal in your life if you just take it one step at a time. And you can always see the next step.

Step Seven

Do something every day that moves you toward your most important goal. When you take an action every day that moves you toward your goal, no matter how small, you eventually develop what is called the Momentum Principle of Success.

You start to move faster and faster toward your goal, and your goal starts to move faster and faster toward you. Perhaps the two most powerful principles for success are *first, get going* and *second, keep going!*

Choose Your Major Goal

Practice the *Ten Goal Method*. Take a clean sheet of paper and write the word *Goals* at the top, along with today's date. Then, write down ten goals you would like to achieve in the next twelve months or so.

The Three P Formula

For the rest of your life, when you write down your goals, always use the three Ps. It seems that your subconscious mind only responds to commands that are phrased in a particular way. They must be *personal, positive,* and in the *present* tense, as though you have already achieved your goal.

Personal means that you use *I* and an action verb for each goal. For example, you say "I earn…," "I drive a…," or "I achieve…"

Write it in the *positive* tense. Instead of saying "I will quit smoking," you say "I am a nonsmoker."

And write it in the *present* tense. Write your goal as though the time has passed and you have already achieved the goal. You are describing it as though it is a current reality.

Double Your Income

If your goal is to double your income, you would select the amount that is double your income and write the goal as "I earn this amount of money each year."

Set a deadline after each of your goal statements. For example, you would say "I earn $XX, XXX by year-end."

Each time you write down your goal in the *personal*, *positive*, *present* tense, it is immediately transferred to your subconscious mind, which then goes to work twenty-four hours a day to help you achieve that goal. Many people have transformed their lives in a very short time by simply sitting down and writing out a series of goals using this process.

Your Major Definite Purpose

Once you have written down ten goals that you would like to accomplish in the next twelve months, you are ready for the next step.

Imagine that you have a *magic wand*. Imagine that you could accomplish all of the goals you have written down sooner or later—if you want them enough and are willing to work for them. But with this magic wand, you could wave it over the page and you could have any one goal on your list within twenty-four hours.

Here's the question: If you could achieve any one goal in life within twenty-four hours, which one would have the greatest positive impact on your life today?

Whatever your answer, this then becomes your *major definite purpose*. It becomes your number one most important goal around which you design your entire life.

You can have a series of different goals, in different areas of your life, but you must always have one goal that is more important than any other.

Achieving Your Biggest Goal

You then take a clean sheet of paper. You write your goal at the top of the page in *personal*, *positive*, *present* tense language and add a deadline.

For example, you could write "I will earn $100,000 by year-end."

You then make a list of everything you can think of that you could possibly do to achieve this goal. What subjects will you have to learn? What problems will you have to overcome? Whose cooperation and assistance will you require? And, especially, what actions will you have to take every day to achieve this goal?

You then take immediate action on your goal. You take the first step by doing at least one thing on your list.

From this day forward, you do something every day that moves you one step closer to your most important goal.

Here is a remarkable discovery. As you begin to work each day toward your major definite purpose, you start to make progress on many of your other goals as well. By focusing on a single goal, you begin to achieve many other goals at the same time.

This process of writing down ten goals, selecting one goal as your major definite purpose, making a plan for its accomplishment, and then doing something every single day will change your life and virtually assure that you hit your bull's-eye, far sooner than you may have ever imagined possible.

Take immediate **ACTION** on your goal. Take the first step by doing at least one thing on your list.

CHAPTER THREE

The Power of Purpose

The deepest craving in human nature is for a sense of meaning and purpose in life. As Mark Twain wrote, "The two most important days in your life are the day you are born and the day you find out why."

You were put on this earth to do something wonderful with your life. What is it? Wayne Dyer wrote, "Each child comes into the world with secret orders." What might yours be?

Each person has a special role to play—a part to fulfill, a reason for living. Spiritually speaking, there are no extra parts in the human building blocks of life. Each person is designed to fit in somewhere, doing something, for someone, in some way.

Abraham Maslow, the groundbreaking psychologist, concluded that people have two types of needs: *deficiency needs* and *being needs*.

Deficiency needs were defined as those fears, doubts, worries, and unresolved conflicts that served as brakes on individual potential and hold people back most of their lives. His conclusion was that fully 98 percent of the population failed to realize their full potential because of one or more of these mental obstacles.

Being needs were defined as the qualities of self-actualizing people—people who felt wonderful about themselves and who were dedicated to becoming more and more of everything they could possibly be.

Maslow's conclusion, and his great contribution to psychology, was that as you free yourself from your deficiency needs, you liberate yourself to fulfill your being needs. As Walt Whitman said, "Keep your face always toward the sunshine—and shadows will fall behind you."

Your Mission Statement

For you to unlock your full potential, to become everything you are capable of becoming, you need a higher purpose for your life. You need to commit yourself to something bigger than yourself. You need the big five: *values*, *vision*, *purpose*, *mission*, and *goals*.

The Big Five

You need *values*, those organizing principles and virtues that are most important to you, and which you will not compromise for any reason. Exceptional men and women are very clear about their values and how those values are practiced in real life. Your values, and the degree to which you stick to those values, form the essence of your character.

You need a *vision*, a clear, exciting picture of your future life as though it was ideal or perfect in every way. The greater clarity you have about your vision for yourself, the more motivated you will be to make that vision a reality, and the faster you will attract that vision into your life.

Your *purpose* and *mission* are the natural extensions of your values and your vision.

And your *goals*. These are the targets you aim for, combined with the step-by-step plans for the activities you need to engage in each day to make your values, vision, purpose, and mission into your reality.

What Is Your Mission in Life?

Most companies spend a lot of time defining their mission statements—why the company exists and how it intends to serve its customers and its community.

A corporate mission statement requires three parts: the mission itself, a method to achieve the mission, and a measure to determine how successful the company is in fulfilling its mission.

Many companies and individuals have mission statements that are vague and unclear and give no guidance or direction about what to do or not to do on a day-to-day basis. For example, according to Steve Jobs, Apple's mission statement was "To put a ding in the universe." What does that mean?

Because of its innovative technology, the company is successful in spite of having a mission statement that is largely meaningless.

A Good Mission Statement

A good business mission statement could be something like "Our mission is to provide our customers with the very best product possible. Our method is to achieve product excellence and to continually improve in every area. Our measure of success is that we grow 25 percent each year in sales and profitability based on customer satisfaction and repeat sales."

With a mission like this, everyone in the company can be clear about their jobs and the goals the company is aiming at. Everyone can be clear about their roles and responsibilities and quickly measure whether they are helping the company to achieve the mission.

A mission is something that can be *accomplished*. You can actually achieve the mission and then shut down and go home. And a six-year-old should be able to tell you what your mission is and how close you are to accomplishing it.

You Need a Personal Mission Statement

My personal mission has not changed in more than thirty years: "My mission is to help people achieve their goals far faster than they would in the absence of my help."

This admittedly awkward mission statement has guided and directed the development, production, and marketing of all of my seminars, workshops, books, audios, and online learning programs throughout my career. I measure the quality and effectiveness of each learning tool or experience I produce by the number of people who use it to improve their life or work.

You can have a personal mission statement for yourself, your family, your community, and you can have a business or career mission for your profession.

Stephen Covey wrote about the importance of having a *family* mission statement, a mission discussed and agreed upon by the family members as the basis of their lives together.

Your Career Mission Statement

Your business or career mission statement could be "I provide excellent services to my customers that enrich and improve their lives and work. My method of achieving this goal is by understanding my customer's needs and practicing continuous and never-ending improvement.

My measure is that my customers and personal income increase by 20 percent or more each year."

What is your mission? What is your mission for each area of your life? The greater clarity you have about your mission—the reason why you are on this earth—the easier it will be for you to hit your bull's-eye in life and to measure your success.

Ask the Right Questions

To determine your mission for the months and years ahead, answer the following questions:

1. Imagine you had all the money you could ever spend, but as a condition of having all this money, you would have to be active and fully engaged in some occupation. What would you choose to do?

2. What do you really love to do? What would you choose to do as work, or with your life, if you were financially independent today?

3. What do you really believe in? What are your deepest values and convictions? What is so important

to you that you want others to share your personal passion, knowledge, and commitment?

4. Who do you really care about? What specific people do you want to help in some way, more than anyone else? What kind of difference do you want to make in your world, if you could make any difference at all?

5. What do you want to be *famous* for? How do you want to be known? What kind of reputation do you want to develop? What do you want people to say about you when you're not there? How do you want to be remembered? What would you want people to say in your obituary or at your funeral?

6. Dale Carnegie once wrote, "The desire for a feeling of importance is one of the chief distinguishing differences between mankind and the animals." What gives you your greatest feeling of importance and personal value?

The most important work you do in life is *thinking*. There is perhaps no area where thinking is more important to your long-term happiness and success than in determining your mission in each of the important areas of your life.

Write Out Your Mission Statement

Take some time to write out your mission statement. This is your real "bull's-eye" in life. It's what you want to accomplish more than anything else. It is the difference you want to make in the lives of other people.

Here is a simple model of a mission statement you can use:

My mission is: _____

Define it in terms of the difference you want to make in the lives of others.

My method to achieve my mission is:_____

Write down the activities you will engage in.

The way I will measure my success in the accomplishment of my mission is: _____

What one number or result could you focus on that would be the best single measure of your success in accomplishing your mission?

Service to Others

You are designed in a special way by the creator to only really feel good about yourself when you are serving other people in some way. Your level of self-esteem and personal value, how much you like yourself, is largely determined by making a greater contribution to the lives of others than whatever it is you are taking out. This is why it says in the Bible, "It is more blessed to give than to receive."

Your rewards will always be determined by your service. If you want to increase the quality and quantity of your rewards, you must increase the quality and quantity of the service you render to other people. Perhaps one of the greatest questions to ask in business, and in life, is: "What can I do to increase the value of my service to others today?"

Wayne Dyer wrote,

"Each child comes
into the world with
secret orders."

**WHAT MIGHT
YOURS BE?**

MY
MISSION:

CHAPTER FOUR
The Power of Concentration

You can only hit your personal bull's-eye when you have clarity, when you focus on your most important goals, and when you concentrate on one thing at a time.

The disciplines of focus and concentration are learnable and must be learned through practice, over and over, until they are locked in as lifelong habits. Johann Wolfgang von Goethe said, "Everything is hard before it is easy."

My friend Ed Foreman said, "Good habits are hard to form but easy to live with. Bad habits are easy to form but hard to live with."

It is difficult to form the habits of focus and concentration, but once you have formed them, they become automatic and easy. In fact, they become easier to practice than the old bad habits of diversion and distraction.

Aristotle said, "We are what we repeatedly do." Fully 95 percent of what we do each day is habitual, automatic, and often unthinking. The key is for you to *form good habits and make them your masters.*

Fortunately, any habit can be learned with practice and repetition every day until it becomes as natural as breathing. **Practice does not make perfect. Practice makes permanent.**

The Attraction of Distraction

There is a major problem in the world of work today that is threatening the careers and the success of millions of people. It is the tendency to be continually distracted by electronic interruptions.

The invention of the cell phone started this mild form of "attention deficit disorder," but the invention of smartphones, Facebook, Twitter, LinkedIn, YouTube, and the millions of apps available to everyone anywhere, at low cost or free, are destroying the ability of people to concentrate on and complete their most important tasks.

Addicted to Distraction

According to neuroscientists, each time you react or respond to a ring, ding, noise, or signal from an electronic device, you perk up with excitement and anticipation. Your brain releases a small shot of dopamine, which is the same chemical contained in cocaine and other stimulants.

As with any drug, once you experience your first shot of dopamine in the morning by checking your email or surfing your social media sites, you quickly become addicted for the entire day. Your thinking patterns and brain begin to change. You slip into the habit of continually checking for messages, and if there aren't any, you send them to different people to stimulate a response and to trigger more shots of dopamine.

Results Are Everything

The most important word for success in business and in personal life is *results*. To get the results required of you, you must start and finish work that is specific, measurable, and time-bound. You must *complete your tasks.*

Task completion is indispensable to your success, and everything that interferes with your ability to start and complete your tasks undermines your potential for success.

The sad news is that millions of people today cannot work for even a few minutes without responding to intellectual interruptions of some kind.

The basic habits of time management, of focus and concentration, require disciplined practice and repetition at the beginning, but afterward they enable you to accomplish vastly more than most of the people around you.

The Personal Management Process

You can dramatically increase your productivity, performance, output, and income when you get your life and work organized. Here's how:

Step One

Become absolutely clear about your goals in each area of your life. Think on paper. Organize your goals in terms of priority, and be clear about your most important goal in each area at each moment of your life.

Step Two

Draw up an overall plan, a checklist to follow, in the completion of any task or project. Every minute spent in planning saves ten minutes in execution.

Practice the Six P Formula: *Proper Prior Preparation Prevents Poor Performance.*

Create a checklist with each task or activity necessary to complete your goal, organized by sequence. Never start work until you have taken a few minutes to prepare this checklist. This gives you a track to run on—a guide to follow.

Step Three

Make lists. List everything you have to do to complete every project in the future. Each month, list the tasks you have to complete that month. Make a list every week, the weekend before.

Most important, make a list every day before you begin work. The best time to make your list is the night before, at the end of the working day. But whatever happens, your very first task at the beginning of each day is to write out a list of everything you have to do that day.

When something new comes up, write it down on the list before you do it, even if it is to return a telephone call or an email. A list gives you a *sense of control* over your day. As you go through your list, ticking off each item, you generate a feeling of forward momentum that both stimulates and motivates you in a positive way.

Step Four

Set priorities on your list before you start work. Use the 80/20 Rule. This rule says that 20 percent of the items on your list will account for 80 percent of your results from the items on that list. Sometimes it is the 90/10 Rule. Sometimes one item on your list is worth more than all the other items put together.

The contest is always between those activities that are "fun and easy" and those activities that are "hard and necessary." The question is always: *Which is going to win?*

The natural tendency for most people is to procrastinate and delay on exactly those tasks and activities that can have the greatest possible consequences for your success and happiness in the future.

Use the **ABCDE** method to organize your list before you begin.

A= Must do. This is an essential task you absolutely must complete to be successful and to stay on top of your work; noncompletion has serious consequences.

B= Should do. This is a task that needs to be done sooner or later, but it is not as important as your A tasks. There are only mild consequences for noncompletion. The rule is that you should never do a B task when you have an A task left undone.

C= Nice to do. This is something pleasant and enjoyable, like chatting with a friend, checking email, or playing with social media. They may be nice to do, but these activities have absolutely no consequences at all for your life. *Rule: Social networking is social not-working.*

D= Delegate. This is a task or activity you can delegate to someone else to free up your time for those tasks only you can do. The rule is to delegate everything possible so you have more time to work on the tasks most important to your career.

E= Eliminate. The rule is that you will never get caught up. You cannot continually seek ways to work more efficiently so that you can do more things. The only way you can get control of your time and your life is to stop doing things. In this sense, perhaps the very best rule is *just say no!*

From now on, just say no to any task or activity that is not the highest and best use of your time.

Practice creative procrastination. This means you deliberately procrastinate on those activities of low value so you have more time available to complete the tasks most important to your career.

How to Set Priorities

There are three questions you can ask when setting priorities for your work:

1. If I could only do one thing all day long, what would be the most valuable task I could do in my work?

2. What can I and only I do that, if done well, can make a real difference?

   This is something that only you can do. If you don't do it, no one else will do it for you. But if you do it and do it well, it can make a positive difference in your career.

3. What is the most valuable use of my time right now?

Asking and answering these questions is the key to excellent time management. Your ability to choose one task, the most important thing you could possibly do at this moment, and then take action on this task is the key to high performance, success, and achievement in life.

Practice Single-Handling

Once you have set your priorities using the above methods, select your number one task and begin on that first thing in the morning, before anything else on your list.

Single-handling, your ability to concentrate on your most important task and stay at it until it is 100 percent complete, is perhaps the most powerful time management technique of all. It requires character, discipline, willpower, and tremendous determination. It is the quality or characteristic of all high-achieving men and women.

Keep On Working

All great achievements in life are preceded by a long period of focus and concentration, sometimes for weeks, months, and even years, before success is achieved. Every big achievement was preceded by hundreds, even thousands of small efforts and activities that no one ever sees or appreciates.

Henry Wadsworth Longfellow wrote:

> "The heights by great men reached and kept were not attained by sudden flight, but they, while their companions slept, were toiling upward in the night."

In its simplest terms, success is the result of *task completion*. In life, you get no points or rewards for partial task completion, even if you complete a task 95 percent. Your reputation for time management, for starting and completing major tasks, soon makes you the go-to person.

BULL'S-EYE

Perhaps the most important ability for success in work is *dependability.* The people around you absolutely know that if they give you a task or responsibility, you will complete it on schedule, on budget, and to a high level of quality. This is the ultimate end and benefit of clarity, focus, and concentration. It is the key to hitting your bull's-eyes in life.

"Everything is hard before it is **EASY**."

— *Johann Wolfgang von Goethe*

CHAPTER FIVE

The Power of Excellence

You will only be really successful and happy when you become excellent at something. What should it be for you?

When I began studying personal success, I stumbled into the world of self-esteem psychology. The basic principle is that your self-esteem, defined as how much you like yourself, largely determines everything that happens to you in life.

Liking Yourself

The more you like yourself, the bigger the goals you will set and the longer you will persist. The more you like yourself, the healthier and happier you will be—physically, mentally, and emotionally. The more you like yourself, the more you like other people and the more they like you in return. The more you like yourself, the more energy you will have and the stronger your immune system will be. The more you like yourself, the more you will find that every part of your life will be better.

The flip side of the coin of self-esteem is called self-efficacy. Self-efficacy, a key part of your self-image and self-esteem, is defined as how competent you feel you are at what you do.

How Good You Are

It seems that self-esteem and self-efficacy reinforce each other. The more you like yourself, the better you do your work or anything else you attempt. The better you do your work, the more you like and respect yourself. Each one feeds the other. Each of them is self-reinforcing. The better you get, the better you do and the better you feel.

Everyone has the ability to be excellent at something and often many things. Your job is to find out what your *area of excellence* is, or should be, and then throw your whole heart into becoming very, very good in that one area.

The Top 20 Percent

When I was twenty-four and struggling, with holes in my shoes and no money in my pockets, I got into a straight commission sales job, cold-calling door-to-door. If I didn't make a sale, I didn't eat. I struggled for many months. Then one day, a top salesman tossed off a statistic to me that changed my life forever.

He said, "Did you know that the top 20 percent of salespeople earn 80 percent of the money in every industry?"

I had never heard that before. I immediately decided that if the top 20 percent earned most of the money, I wanted to be in the top 20 percent. This decision changed my life.

You Can Do It

Then came the disillusion and discouragement. I had not graduated from high school and had worked at laboring jobs for several years. I had never been good at anything. I never got good grades, and I was never chosen to play on any teams in junior high or high school. I was not even very good as a door-to-door salesman.

Yet there I was, with the grand notion of being in the top 20 percent of my field. I had never been in the top 20 percent of anything.

Everyone Starts at the Bottom

Then I learned something that changed my life and removed my feelings of discouragement and low self-esteem. I learned that everyone in the top 20 percent today started in the bottom 80 percent.

Everyone doing well once did poorly. Everyone at the front of the buffet line of life started at the back of the line. Everyone at the top of career fields today was, at one time, not even in that field at all and may not even have known it existed.

As T. Harv Eker says, "Every master was once a disaster."

What the Numbers Mean

A major insurance company studied the income of five thousand of its agents to see if this 80/20 Rule applied. What they discovered was that it was true: the top 20 percent of their agents were earning 80 percent of the commissions they paid out each year.

But when they calculated what this difference meant, they were truly surprised. They found that the average income of the salespeople in the top 20 percent was sixteen times the average income of the people in the bottom 80 percent. (You can do this calculation for yourself.)

The 1 Percent versus the 99 Percent

There has been a good deal of controversy over the 1 percent versus the 99 percent. Some people say the top 1 percent of earners in our society earn more than the other 99 percent. However, when you study the numbers, you find that it is actually the 3 percent versus the 97 percent.

It is the 3 percent of people with clear, written goals and plans that they work on every day who eventually end up earning more than the other 97 percent put together.

Even better, it is the 20 percent versus the 80 percent. In every field, the top 20 percent end up earning 80 percent of the money and controlling 80 percent of the wealth.

The Real Question

The real question should not be wealth distribution. The real question should be, since almost everyone starts at the bottom, with limited education, skills, or money, how is it that certain people rise to the top and earn ten or twenty times the amount of the same people they started with—with the same levels of intelligence, education, contacts, and opportunities?

In fact, according to a study by the Associated Press, the average income of Fortune 500 CEOs is 257 times the average income of the people who work in those corporations. How did these top executives, who started off their careers in their early twenties, reach the point where they are earning 257 times the amount of money as some of the people they started out with, at the same starting line?

The Simple Answer

The answer is simple: the high earners have invested many years of hard work in becoming absolutely excellent at the most important things they do and at achieving the most important results required by their corporations.

What this means is that income inequality is largely self-determined. You largely decide the amount you earn from your work over the course of your career. The amount you earn is determined by the things you do, continually upgrading your skills, becoming better at those tasks that enable you to get the results people are willing to pay you for.

Income Gap versus Skills Gap

The late Gary S. Becker, the 1992 Nobel Prize–winning economist at the University of Chicago, asserted that there is more of a skills gap in America than an income gap—those people with the skills that are most in demand are always employed and well-paid while those who lack the necessary skills earn far less and are often unemployed.

Today, young people graduating from college with STEM qualifications (Science, Technology, Engineering, and Mathematics) are being snapped up by large corporations and are sometimes offered more than $100,000 for their first year. Students graduating with liberal arts degrees lag behind with starting salaries less than half that amount.

The Key to High Income

Dr. K. Anders Ericsson of Florida State University is the world's leading authority on elite performance. His twenty-five years of research into the career paths of highly paid executives shows that they all engaged in a process he calls deliberate practice.

What this means is that high earners are focused on developing one skill at a time, clearly and deliberately, throughout their careers. The net result of developing and mastering one key skill at a time, and then combining these key skills with their repertoire of other key skills, was that they became more and more valuable, eventually earning ten times, twenty times, one hundred times, even 257 times more than the same people they started off with at the beginning of their careers.

Failure to Improve

According to Ericsson, people in the bottom 80 percent will work during their first year of employment to learn their particular job or craft. After that, they slow down, level off, and never get any better. They don't read any books, listen to any audio programs, or take any additional courses. They simply flatten out.

After ten years of work, they are no more productive than they were after one year. Their salaries reflect this lack of increased productivity. Their incomes go up (as long as they are employed) at an average of about 1 percent per year over inflation.

The High Earners

But the people in the top 20 percent, those who continue to learn, grow, and improve in their jobs, enjoy income increases that can average 11 percent per year. If your income goes up 11 percent per year, it doubles every 6.5 years.

At that rate, a person starting work at $50,000 a year will be earning more than $400,000 in twenty years! As the saying goes, "The most powerful force in the universe is compound interest."

Increase Your Income

So, how do you get onto this gravy train of higher and higher income throughout your working lifetime? The answer is so simple, and borne out by more than twenty-five years of research, that it is actually embarrassing.

It is this: You take one step at a time. You improve one skill at a time. You become excellent throughout your career by mastering the one skill that can be the most helpful to you at that moment.

Here's the key question that largely determines your success or failure, and your income, in your career: *What one skill, if I developed it and did it in an excellent fashion consistently, would have the greatest positive impact on my career?*

Use Your Magic Wand

Imagine again that you could wave a magic wand and overnight become absolutely excellent at any one skill in your field. What one skill, if you were excellent at it, could help you the most to double your income? What one skill could enable you to get better results than anything else you could learn to do? What one skill would accelerate your career faster than any other skill?

To answer this question, you require our three old friends: *clarity*, *focus*, and *concentration*. You must be clear about the one skill that can help you the most. You must focus single-mindedly on the development of that skill. You must concentrate an average of two hours a day, five days per week, or even more, on the development of that skill to a higher level. If you do this, your future is virtually guaranteed.

Analyze Your Situation

Think about your major definite purpose, your single most important goal in life, and ask this question: *What one skill, if I developed it and did it in an excellent fashion consistently, would help me the most to achieve my most important goal?*

As motivational speaker Les Brown says, "To achieve something you have never achieved before, you must become someone you have never been before."

We can paraphrase that by saying, **"To *achieve a goal* that you have never achieved before, you must *develop a skill* you've never had before."**

Developing a Skill

How do you climb a ladder? One step at a time. Imagine that when climbing a ladder, your left hand and left foot are knowledge and your right hand and right foot are skill.

To climb the ladder of success in your career, you need both hands and both feet. You need to develop knowledge with one side and skill with the other.

Each rung on the ladder of skill development increases your *earning ability*, your value to your organiza- tion, and the amount of money they will pay you to get results.

If you keep developing new skills, one at a time, you keep becoming more valuable, and your company or some other company will willingly pay you to get the results you can achieve for them.

Keep Learning and Growing

Once you have mastered the key skill you have identi-
fied, then what do you do? Simple—you ask the question
again. *What one skill will help me the most to move ahead
faster in my career?*

Once you have decided upon the most important
skill you can develop, turn it into a goal with a plan.
Write it down clearly in a *personal*, *positive*, *present* tense
with a deadline.

For example, you could write "I am absolutely excellent at this skill by this date."

Make a Plan for Excellence

You can then make a list of everything you can do to
learn and practice to develop this skill. Organize this
list into a plan by sequence and priority. Take action on
your plan immediately by doing something every day to
develop this skill.

Wonderfully enough, as you focus on the development of the one skill that can help you the most at this

time, you start to improve in your other skills. When you decide to become a lifelong learner, you automatically find yourself learning and improving in other areas, almost as if by osmosis.

Continuous Improvement

The key to lifelong learning is for you to practice **CANEI**, which stands for:

Continuous
And
Never-**E**nding
Improvement.

Never stop getting better. Constantly seek out new ways to improve your efficiency and effectiveness. Feed your mind with new ideas, methods, and techniques. Learn new skills as if your career depended upon it—because it does.

All Skills Are Learnable

There are two final points in your development of excellence. First, all skills are *learnable*. You can learn any skill you need to learn to advance your career. There are no limits.

Second, you could be only one skill away from doubling your productivity, performance, output, results, and income. Sometimes just one skill, added to your existing toolbox of skills, can enable you to achieve extraordinary results, far beyond your imagination today. What could it be?

You will only be really **SUCCESSFUL** and **HAPPY** when you become **EXCELLENT** at something.

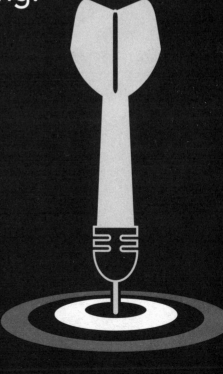

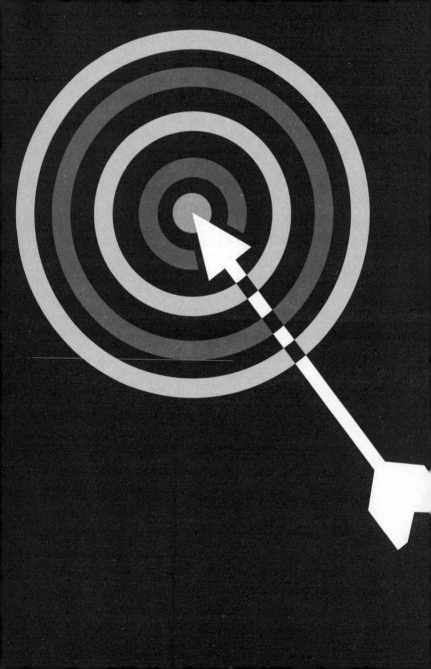

CHAPTER SIX

The Power of People

Your success will largely be determined by the people you know and the people who know you in a positive way. The formula is QR × QR = QL. (The quality of your relationships multiplied by the quantity of your relationships equals the quality of your life).

By now, you are clear about your values, purpose, mission, goals, and priorities. Now, it is time for you to make up a list of all the people whose assistance and cooperation you will require to achieve your goal.

Make a List

Begin with your family and friends. Include your boss and coworkers. Think about outside colleagues, your bank, your suppliers, and other people who can be of assistance to you. Think on paper.

How can you respond to each person's favorite radio channel? This is WIIFM, or What's in It for Me?

If you are in sales, entrepreneurship, or business of any kind, you can ask WIIFMC, which stands for What's in It for My Customer?

Today, because of the incredible competition for customers and the limited attention that customers can pay to you and your message, you have to practice "give to get."

You must become a "go-giver" rather than a "go-getter."

Put In Before You Take Out

There seem to be two types of people in our society today, especially in those areas where money, status, fame, and success are concerned. There are people who see others as tools to be manipulated, people from whom they can gain something to their advantage.

The other way of looking at people is to see them as unique individuals with wants, needs, and personalities that make them valuable within their own right.

The first type of person, when they meet or even hear about someone new, is always asking, "What can I get from this person?"

Think the Way Top People Think

But the top people have a different attitude. They ask, "What can I give to this person that they want, need, and appreciate that might be the beginning of a positive relationship?"

It seems that at every turning point in your life, a person will be standing there. When you look back over your life, beginning as a teenager, you will note that individuals you may have forgotten about had a major impact on the person you are today and on everything you have accomplished.

Network Regularly

Going back to the Law of Probability, which we discussed earlier, one of the most productive things you can do is network with as many different people as possible throughout your life and your career.

The bottom 80 percent of people in our society, those whose income has flattened out, who suffer job insecurity, and who are frustrated with their lives, usually go home every night and watch television or socialize with their friends.

The top 20 percent of people, on the other hand, are continually seeking out opportunities to network and interact with other people they might be able to help and who might be able to help them in turn.

One Person Can Make a Difference

Some years ago, I was speaking at a seminar for a national corporation. My talk was in the morning. The previous speaker decided to stay over an extra night so he could meet me and hear me speak.

At that time, I had an ache in my left ankle that was causing me to limp a little. He noticed and asked me about it, then went back to his room and brought me a bottle of tablets that had been specially formulated for this type of joint pain. It was his personal supply, but he gave it to me and wished me luck.

Take an Interest in Others

On a whim, I asked him, "How is everything going for you in your career?"

We started talking, and it turned out that his biggest concern at that time was a real estate investment he had made in Massachusetts, just outside of Boston. He was in way over his head and did not know how to get out from under this burden.

We were in Fort Lauderdale, Florida. Some years before, I had worked with a real estate entrepreneur from Boston who now lived in Coral Gables. I picked up my phone, called him, and explained the situation.

One Call Away

As it happened, my friend was quite familiar with the real estate development that this speaker was involved in. He made a couple calls and put my friend in contact with a developer who was working on lands adjacent to these lands in Massachusetts. I learned later that over the next nine months, they were able to refinance the land, sell it, and relieve my speaker friend's financial stress.

You Never Know

When I thought back on that situation, I was amazed at how this small act of networking had worked out. The speaker brought me a small bottle of tablets for my ankle, and I learned about his problem and was able to put him together with exactly the right person who could help to save his financial life.

The point is that you never know how or when someone can help you, nor do they know how and when you may help them. You must simply use the Law of Probability and keep expanding your network as wide as you can. As they say in fishing, cast a broad net.

Be a Joiner

Join your local business clubs and associations. Attend regularly. Get involved. Meet other people. But instead of looking for what they can do for you, look for something you can do for them.

When you meet a new person, rather than talking about yourself and shoving your business card into their hand, ask them about themselves and what sort of work they are doing. Especially ask them what you would need to know to send them a new customer.

Help Them First

The very best way to build friends and contacts in business is to look for ways to help other people to improve their sales and profitability. You will often be amazed at how the most casual contact that you reach out to with the offer of a favor or kindness of some kind can turn into a major turning point in your life or business.

When you meet a new person, make it a habit to respond immediately to that person in some way. Send them an email telling them how much you enjoyed meeting them and that you look forward to seeing them again. Attach a favorite article or piece of information to your email that might be helpful to the other person. Even better, send a handwritten thank-you card to the new acquaintance telling them how much you enjoyed meeting them.

Large Things Grow from Small Seeds

Many years ago, I read an article by the president of a large organization discussing an issue in which I had considerable interest. I immediately sat down and wrote this executive a letter, agreeing with his recommendations in the article and expressing the hope that someday we would cross paths when I was in his part of the country.

About three years later, I was at a large national meeting and ran into this gentleman. He still remembered me from the letter. We began talking and eventually had lunch and dinner together. That chance meeting led to one of the closest and best personal friendships of my life, now going on more than twenty-five years.

The Success Principle

One of my favorite success principles is "the more you give of yourself with no expectation of return, the more that will come back to you from the most unexpected sources."

When you do a kindness or a favor for another person, you may never see that person again, but through some miracle of the universe, someone will appear to do a kindness or a favor for you, exactly when you need it.

The Bible says, "Whatever one sows, that will he also reap."

When you sow seeds of helpfulness, friendliness, kindness, and generosity, you are doing your part. You do not have to worry where your benefits or returns will come from. Your job is to take care of the sowing. Nature and nature's God will take care of the reaping.

Make People Feel Important

Mary Kay Ash, the founder of Mary Kay Cosmetics, one of the most successful network marketing companies in the world, was famous for saying that you should imagine that every person you meet has a sign around their neck that reads "Make me feel important."

This is the secret of excellent relationships with other people.

Seven Great Behaviors

There are seven behaviors you can practice with each new person you meet and with all the people in your life. When you practice these behaviors, you will be amazed at how the quality of your life improves:

1. **Never criticize, condemn, or complain about people or their behaviors.** Even if you disapprove, keep your opinions to yourself. As Frank Sinatra sang, "If you can't say anything real nice, it's better not to talk at all, is my advice."

   Most people's conversations tend to be negative. They complain about a variety of things in their lives. They condemn people and situations for causing them problems and concerns. They criticize everyone around them with whom they disagree. They develop genuinely negative personalities.

Don't join in. If other people speak in negative ways, you don't need to chip in. Simply listen quietly and then go on your way. Don't throw fuel on the fire.

2. **Be agreeable.** The most popular people everywhere are people who are genuinely agreeable and friendly, no matter what is going on. Even if they disagree with you, they don't express it. Instead, they may ask questions to try to understand your position, but they are generally cheerful most of the time.

Very often, there will be situations where you have arguments or disagreements with other people. But in most cases, these arguments or disagreements are not important. Ask yourself, "What's important here?"

If it's not really important, just let it go. Be cheerful, open, and friendly. Be the positive type of person other people want to be around.

3. **Practice acceptance.** Each person has a deep need to be unconditionally accepted by the other people in their lives. When you satisfy this need by practicing acceptance with each person you meet, you improve their self-image, raise their self-esteem, make them feel better about themselves, and cause them to like and respect you even more.

   And how do you express acceptance? Simple— just smile. Whenever you smile at another person, you are bathing them in acceptance and paying them value. When you smile at a person, it makes them feel attractive and important. It raises their self-esteem. And all it takes is a smile.

4. **Express appreciation**. One of the most powerful ways to make a person feel important and to raise their self-esteem is to appreciate them for the large and small things they do.

   And how do you express appreciation? Simple— just say thank-you. Say thank-you to everyone you live or work with for everything they do, small or large.

Whenever you thank a person, they feel good about themselves, and as a result, they feel good about you. In addition, they want to do more of those things for which you are thanking them, so they can again trigger your response and the positive feelings that go with it.

5. **Express admiration.** Abraham Lincoln said, "Everybody likes a compliment."

Look for things to compliment and admire in others. Compliment them on their clothing, their personal possessions, and their hairstyle. Compliment them on their home, their car, and any of their possessions. Compliment them on their accomplishments and the look of their offices or workplace.

Each time you compliment a person, you make them feel more valuable and important. As a result, they like you more and are more open to cooperating with you. And you can always find something you like about another person or about their possessions or achievements.

6. **Express approval.** Praise and approval satisfy one of the deepest needs in human nature—the need to feel valuable. Whenever you praise people for anything, their self-esteem goes up immediately. They feel better about themselves. They like and respect you more as well.

   Praise people for large and small accomplishments. Praise people regularly when they do anything that is positive and productive in your eyes.

   One of the most powerful ways to motivate staff members or children is to continually praise them when they do something right. At the same time, refuse to criticize or complain when they make a mistake.

7. **Pay attention.** One of the most powerful ways to make people feel valuable and important is to listen to them intently when they talk. Face them directly, lean slightly forward, and hang on every word they say.

   Imagine that your eyes are sun lamps and you want to give the other person's face a tan. Bathe their whole face, especially their mouth and lips, with the warmth of your eyes.

In effective listening, you should listen without interrupting or making any attempt to interrupt. Pause before replying to show that you are carefully considering what the person has just said.

8. **Question for clarification.** Ask "How do you mean?" if there is any possibility of misunderstanding. Remember, the person who asks questions has control. The more you ask questions and listen intently to the answers, the more the other person will like and trust you and feel comfortable in your presence.

9. **Finally, in conversation, feed back what the other person has said in your own words.** This is the real "acid test" of listening. When you can paraphrase their comments in your own words, it shows the person you were really paying attention. When you go through life looking for ways to expand your contacts, seeking ways to help people before you ask them to help you, and making people feel important, they will line up to help you achieve your goals and hit your bull's-eye.

The formula is
QR × QR = QL

the **QUALITY** of your **RELATIONSHIPS**

multiplied by

the **QUANTITY** of your **RELATIONSHIPS**

equals

the **QUALITY** of your **LIFE** 💘

CHAPTER SEVEN

The Power of Persistence

Your ability and willingness to persist in the face of all setbacks and adversity is the most important single guarantor of your ultimate success.

When you set big goals for yourself, the one thing you can be sure of is that you will immediately run into storms and headwinds. Often, immediately after setting a big goal, your life will go into a period of turbulence, and a series of unexpected setbacks and difficulties will occur. This is all to be expected.

Set a Big Goal

One of my students set a goal in my seminar to double his income within six months. When he went to work on Monday, they announced the company was shutting down and he was being laid off, as was everyone else.

He said to himself, "This is great! I set a goal to double my income, and now I'm unemployed."

Later that week, his wife was out shopping, and she ran into an old friend of hers from school. As they chatted, the old friend said that her husband had just started a new business and was looking for a top salesman to sell their new product. The wife of the man from my seminar said that her husband was excellent in sales and he just happened to be available. Could they set up a meeting?

A Blessing in Disguise

The bottom line was that this man went to the interview that Friday and got the job. He started work the following Monday. The product was excellent, the company was successful, and within two months, he was earning twice as much as he had ever earned in his life.

He realized in retrospect that if he had not lost his previous job, he never would have been available to take a job where he actually achieved his goal. This sort of thing will happen to you as well.

Bounce Back from Adversity

One of the measures of your character is how well you respond to adversity—how resilient you are and how quickly you bounce back from unexpected difficulties.

Napoleon Hill said, **"Persistence is to the character of man as carbon is to steel."**

You never really know what you are made of deep down inside until you face what appear to be insurmountable problems. But the good news is that nature never sends you a problem too big for you to solve.

There is no such thing as failure, only feedback.

Character Development

There are some powerful and proven techniques you can incorporate into your worldview to deal with the inevitable short-term failures and difficulties you will experience:

1. **Stay calm**. Take a deep breath and just relax. When you become emotional or upset, your neocortex, your thinking brain where you reason and decide, shuts down.

When you are angry or worried, you fall back on your amygdala, your animal brain responsible for the fight-or-flight reaction. In this state, you are much more likely to make bad decisions and choices and to say or do the wrong things. Instead, stay calm.

2. **Get the facts.** No situation is ever as bad as it initially appears. Even if it is, be sure to get the facts before you respond. Ask questions. What exactly happened? How exactly did it happen? Who was involved? How can we be sure?

   You will often find that you are misinformed. You heard of something that turned out not to be true or was only partially true.

   The more you ask questions, as top people do, the longer you remain calm and in complete control of your thinking and your emotions. It is very hard to ask questions and become upset at the same time.

3. **Look for the good in every situation.** Some of your greatest successes in life will originally appear to be setbacks or problems that could have caused you a great deal of stress and anxiety.

When you look back on your life's experience, you will find that losing a job or a relationship, or even going broke in a business, contained valuable insights and ideas that enabled you to be successful and happy later in life.

There Is Always Something Good

After interviewing five hundred of the most successful people in contemporary history over a period of twenty-two years, Napoleon Hill came to this conclusion: "Every adversity, every failure, every heartache carries with it the seed of an equal or greater benefit."

Your job is to find it. Whenever W. Clement Stone faced a problem, he would immediately neutralize it by saying, "That's good!" Then, he and the people around him would go to work to find something good in the setback or difficulty that had occurred.

Here is a wonderful discovery. If you look for the good in any situation, you will always find something good. Sometimes, the good you find will have far more benefits or advantages than anything you might have lost.

4. **Seek the valuable lesson in every difficulty or temporary failure**. This is one of the greatest success secrets of all. Difficulties come not to obstruct, but to instruct.

    Develop the habit of dealing with each problem with the complete confidence that it contains a valuable lesson that you can use to be more successful in the future.

Your Biggest Problem?

What is your biggest problem in your life today? Everyone has a series of problems they are working on, but everyone also has one big problem that causes them more worry, concern, or frustration than any other. What is yours?

Now, imagine that this problem has been sent to you as a gift to teach you a valuable lesson you need to learn so you can be happier and more successful in the future.

Look for the Gift

Norman Vincent Peale said, "When God wants to send you a gift, he wraps it up in a problem. The bigger the problem he wraps it up in, the bigger the gift that it contains."

What is the gift—the valuable lesson wrapped up inside the biggest problem or difficulty you are wrestling with today? Wonderfully enough, if you look for the gift or valuable lesson, you will always find it.

In fact, if it is big enough or a long-lasting enough problem or difficulty, it may contain several gifts. And the more you examine the problem and seek the gifts, the more gifts you will uncover.

Learn from Your Mistakes

I went through a difficult business situation some years

ago. When it was over, I had lost a good deal of money and sleepless nights. I sat down with a piece of paper. At the top of the page, I wrote: *What lessons have I learned from this situation?*

I then disciplined myself to write down twenty different lessons I had learned from that major business problem. Those lessons served to help and guide me in countless business situations in the months and years that followed. Those lessons helped me to make good decisions and recoup all my losses.

There is nothing wrong with making mistakes in life. They are inevitable and unavoidable. The only wrong thing is not to learn from the mistakes. You want to extract every possible bit of insight and piece of knowledge you possibly can so you don't make those same mistakes again.

1. **Accept responsibility for the problem, whatever it is.** Don't fall into the "loser's trap" of flailing around and blaming everybody and everything for

something that has happened. Instead, simply say, "I am responsible."

Even if you are not responsible for what happened, you are responsible for the way you respond to what happened. By accepting responsibility and refusing to blame anyone or anything for what has happened, you remain calm and positive. You remain in control of the situation. Your mind functions at its very best to help you solve the problem or resolve the difficulty.

2. **Be solution oriented**. One of the characteristics of top people is that they think about solutions most of the time. They recognize that life will be an endless succession of problems, like waves from the ocean that never stop. Therefore, they decide not to become or remain upset about problems. Instead, they look for and focus on the solutions. They are constantly thinking in terms of actions they can take to solve the problem, remove the roadblock, and start moving ahead.

3. **Preprogram your mind.** One of the most important lessons I ever learned was that you have the ability to preprogram your mind so you respond in a particular way when the situation arises.

   For example, you can decide in advance that no matter what happens, you will never give up. You will persist until you succeed. You will try a variety of different things, but you will not stop until you ultimately achieve your goal.

Like an Alarm Clock

Once you have programmed yourself in this way and you face adversity or failure of any kind, you will automatically react like an alarm clock going off and find yourself bouncing back from the initial shock and disappointment. You will automatically feel resilient and positive. Ultimately, you will become *unstoppable*.

There is a powerful method of problem solving and decision making used at the highest levels of business and government. It is both simple and powerful:

First, define the problem clearly. Fully 50 percent of problems can be solved immediately if you can define them clearly in the first place.

Then ask, "What else is the problem?"

Beware of any problem for which there is only one definition. The more ways you can define a particular problem, the more likely it is that you will find the right definition that leads to the correct solution.

Once you have decided exactly what the problem is, ask, "What is the solution?"

Again, beware of a problem for which there is only one solution. Once you have developed a solution, ask, "What else is the solution?"

There is a direct relationship between the number of possible solutions you generate and consider and the quality of the solution you ultimately choose and implement. Quantity of solutions leads to quality of decision making.

Worst Possible Outcome

One of the ways to minimize or eliminate worry associated with a problem or difficulty and regain calmness and clarity is for you to fill out the "disaster report."

First, define the problem clearly, preferably in writing. The act of writing out a clear definition of the problem dramatically clarifies your thinking and makes the problem more amenable to a solution.

Second, ask, "What is the worst possible outcome of this problem?" What is the worst thing that could happen? Then, be open and honest and deal directly with the worst thing that could happen in this problem situation.

Third, resolve to accept the worst, should it occur.

At this point, a most amazing thing happens to you. Once you have defined the worst possible outcome, and you have resolved to accept this, should it occur, your worry drops away. All your stress and tension evaporates. You once again feel calm, collected, and in complete control.

Fourth, begin immediately to improve upon the worst. Begin immediately to do everything you possibly can to make sure that the worst possible outcome does not occur.

This four-step method is really quite phenomenal. You can use it when you face any problem or difficulty in any part of your life. Define the problem clearly, determine the worst possible outcome, resolve to accept the worst should it occur, and then get busy improving upon the worst to make sure that it doesn't happen.

Eliminate Worry and Stress

Finally, to eliminate worry and develop persistence, get so busy working on your goal that you don't have time to worry about your problems or difficulties. The only real cure for worry is persistent, continuous action in the direction of your most important goal.

For you to hit your bull's-eyes in life, you must be perfectly clear about what they are—your goals. You must have plans of activity that you work on every day. You must focus and concentrate on the most important things you can do to achieve your most important goals. You must resolve to persist until you succeed. You must make the decision in advance that, no matter what happens, you will never give up.

BULL'S-EYE

If you do these things over and over again, you will develop the lifelong habit of high achievement. You will accomplish more in the next few months than many people accomplish in several years. Good luck!

GO! Achieve all of the wonderful things that are **POSSIBLE.**

About the Author

 Brian Tracy is the chairman of Brian Tracy International, a human resources development company headquartered in Solana Beach, California. He has written seventy books and produced more than eight hundred audio and video training programs. His materials have been translated into forty languages and used in sixty-four countries. He is active in community affairs and serves as a consultant to several nonprofit organizations.

Brian is also one of the top professional speakers and trainers in the world today. He addresses more than 250,000 men and women each year on the subjects of leadership, strategy, sales, and personal and business success. He has given more than five thousand talks and seminars to five million people worldwide, bringing a unique blend of humor, insight, information, and inspiration.

Brian lives with his wife, Barbara, and their four children in Solana Beach, California, and is an avid student of business, psychology, management, sales, history, economics, politics, metaphysics, and religion. He believes that each person has extraordinary untapped potential that he or she can learn to access and, in so doing, accomplish more in a few years than the average person does in a lifetime.